KU-049-834

EGYPTIAN
Activity Book

Winky Adam

DOVER PUBLICATIONS, INC.
Mineola, New York

NOTE

Ancient Egyptians left behind magnificent art and artifacts which give us a colorful picture of life long ago. In this book, you'll find entertaining mazes, word searches, and dot-to-dot puzzles that make it fun to learn about this long vanished civilization. Puzzle solutions begin on page 55. But no fair peeking!

Bibliographical Note

Egyptian Activity Book is a new work, first published by Dover Publications, Inc. in 1998.

International Standard Book Number: 0-486-40079-4

Manufactured in the United States of America
Dover Publications, Inc., 31 East 2nd Street, Mineola, N.Y. 11501

END

START

Help the god Anubis find
his way back to his temple.

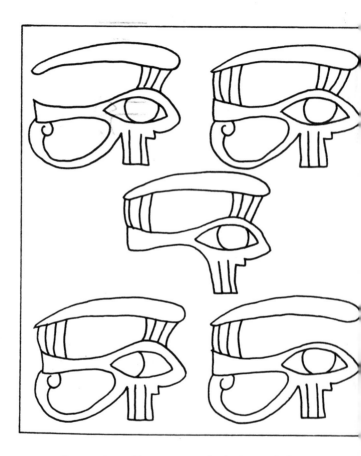

In ancient Egypt people believed that
the Wadjet eye brought good luck.
These amulets, or lucky charms, look

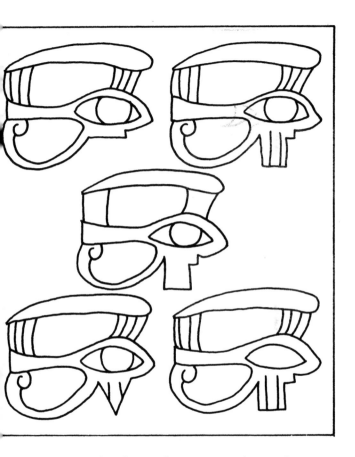

similar, but only two are identical.
Can you find and circle them?

P	H	T	U	L	F	W	O
C	E	R	T	A	B	L	E
V	A	F	S	Q	A	M	G
X	D	I	V	S	U	J	W
S	R	F	C	H	A	I	R
E	E	Z	D	K	P	Q	C
Y	S	L	B	I	J	V	W
S	T	O	O	L	M	T	E

TABLE

Only wealthy Egyptians had furniture like
this in their homes. Find and circle the

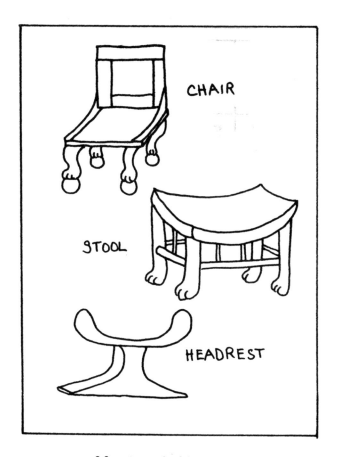

CHAIR

STOOL

HEADREST

names of furniture hidden in the puzzle.
Example: table.

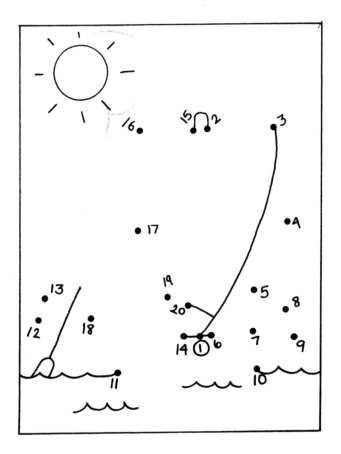

To get from place to place, ancient Egyptians traveled up and down the Nile River. Connect the dots to see an ancient Egyptian ship.

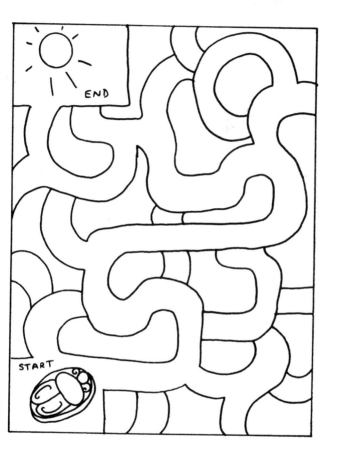

Ancient Egyptians believed that
the scarab beetle rolled the sun across
the sky every day. Help this sacred
bug find his way back to his job!

9

These two mummy cases look the same, but there are 10 differences. Can you spot them?

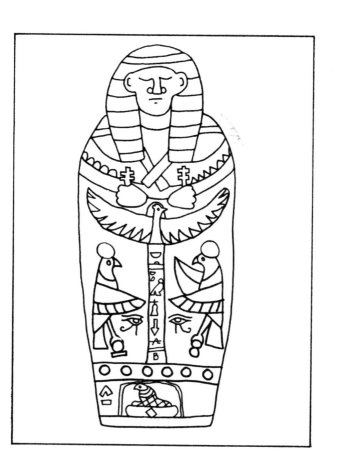

11

Pets were beloved in ancient Egypt. Here
are pictures of some animals that might

have been pets. They are clues to help
you complete the crossword puzzle.

START

Help King Khufu get back to
the great Pyramid at Giza.

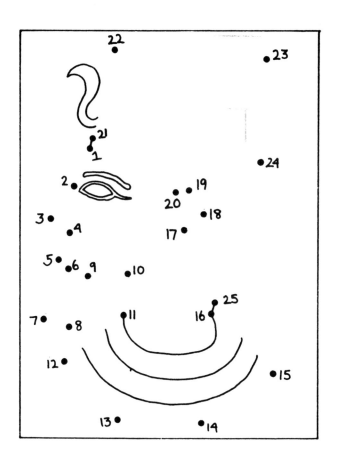

Connect the dots to see a picture
of Hatshepsut, the first woman
pharaoh of Egypt.

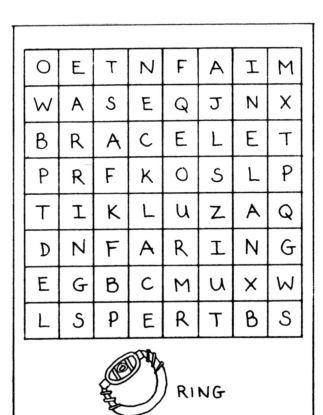

O	E	T	N	F	A	I	M
W	A	S	E	Q	J	N	X
B	R	A	C	E	L	E	T
P	R	F	K	O	S	L	P
T	I	K	L	U	Z	A	Q
D	N	F	A	R	I	N	G
E	G	B	C	M	U	X	W
L	S	P	E	R	T	B	S

RING

Ancient Egyptians loved to wear jewelry made of gold and semi-precious stones.

NECKLACE

BRACELET

EARRINGS

Find the names of the jewelry
hidden in the puzzle.

Here are 8 ceramic hippos that look alike.
Only two are identical. Can you find them?

19

The great Nile has flooded! Help this boat
sail back to its home port in Alexandria.

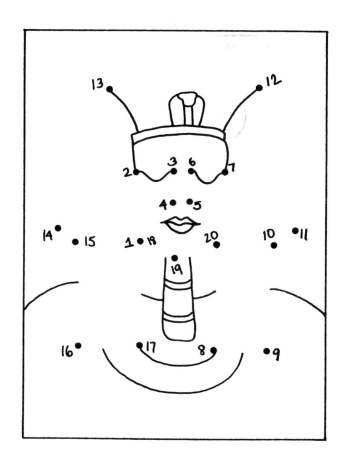

Connect the dots to see a picture of
the powerful pharaoh, Ramses II.

Ancient Egyptians placed the internal
organs of mummies in canopic jars.
Here are 8 jars that look similar. Only 2

**are exactly alike. Can you find
and circle them?**

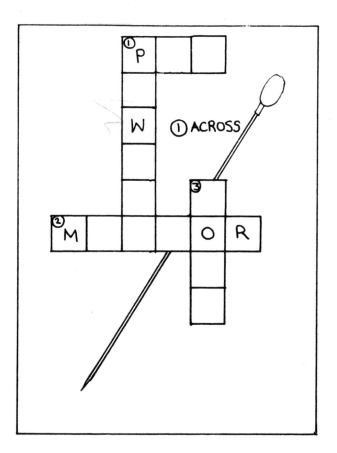

Pictured here are 4 items that might have been used by a woman in ancient Egypt to

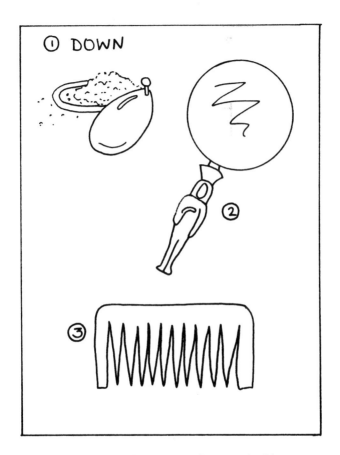

① DOWN

②

③

look her best. They are clues to help you
solve the crossword puzzle.

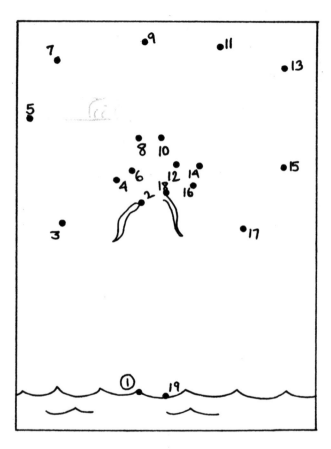

In ancient times, paper was made from
the papyrus reed. Connect the dots
to see a picture of papyrus.

END

START

Help the high priestess find the
great stone Sphinx at Giza.

**There are 10 differences between these
two war scenes of King Tutankhamen.
Can you find and circle them?**

29

This tomb painting depicts a hunting scene.
But wait! There are 12 clues that tell us

that this painting cannot be from ancient
Egypt. Can you find and circle them?

The 8 statues of the cat goddess Bastet
look similar, but only two are identical.
Can you find and circle them?

33

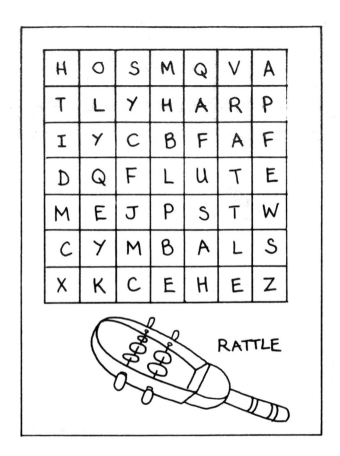

H	O	S	M	Q	V	A
L	L	Y	H	A	R	P
I	Y	C	B	F	A	F
D	Q	F	L	U	T	E
M	E	J	P	S	T	W
C	Y	M	B	A	L	S
X	K	C	E	H	E	Z

RATTLE

Ancient Egyptians loved to play music.
The names of instruments from

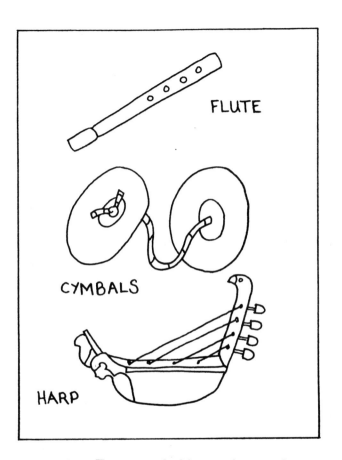

FLUTE

CYMBALS

HARP

ancient Egypt are hidden in the puzzle.
Can you find and circle them?

Here are 6 drawings of the goddess Isis
that look the same. Only two are exactly
alike. Can you find them?

These two painted coffins look similar, but
they are not exactly alike. Find and
circle 10 differences.

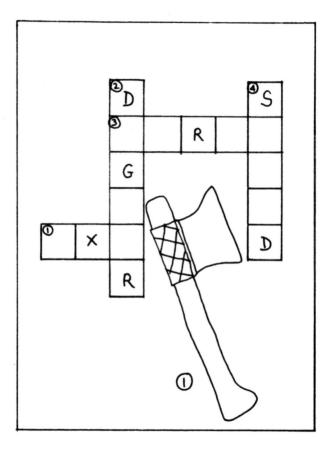

Here are pictures of ancient Egyptian weapons. They are clues to help you finish the crossword puzzle.

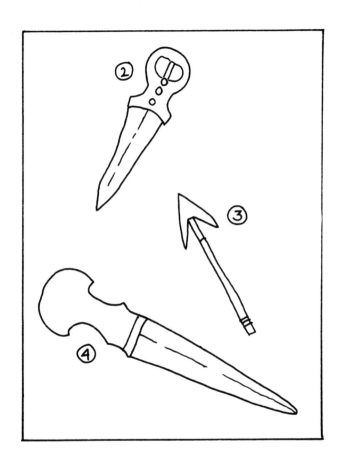

Here are 2 pictures of the sun god, Ra.
They look identical, but there are 10
differences. Can you spot all of them?

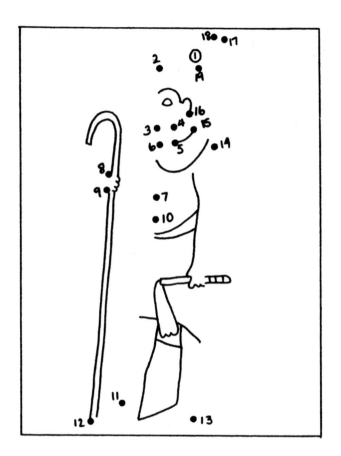

Connect the dots to reveal a golden
statue of an ancient Egyptian king.

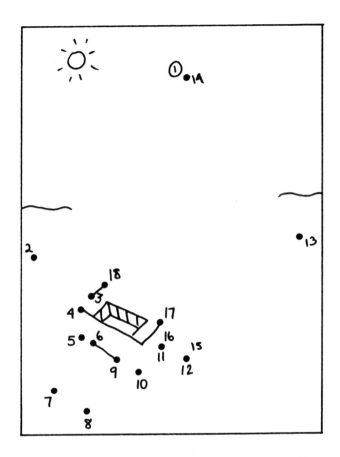

Connect the dots to see the great Pyramid
and the mortuary temple of King Khufu.

Children in ancient Egypt loved to have fun,
just as you do! Here are pictures of some

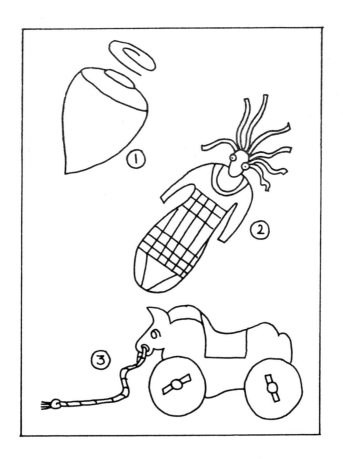

ancient Egyptian toys. They are clues to
help you fill in the crossword puzzle.

Here are 2 wall paintings from an ancient
Egyptian tomb. They look alike, but there

are 12 differences between them.
Find and circle all 12!

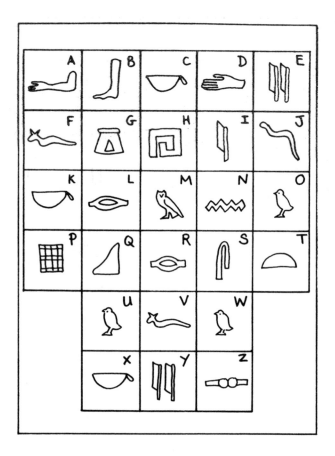

Ancient Egyptians wrote their alphabet
using symbols called hieroglyphs.
Each hieroglyph stands for a sound.

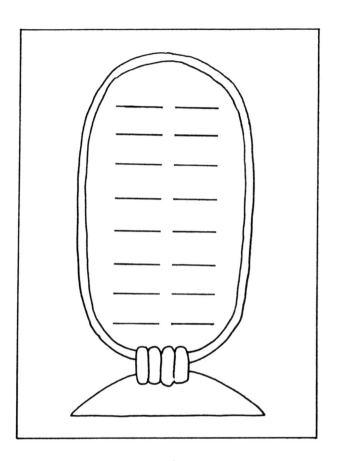

Use the chart shown here to write your name. Start at the top and work down.

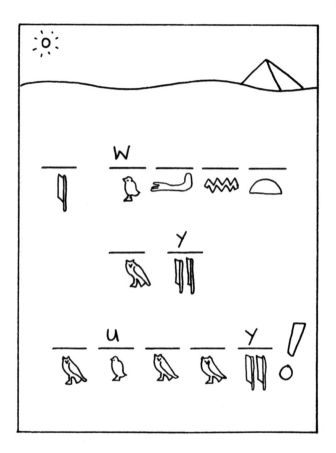

Use the hieroglyph chart on page 50 to
fill in the blanks and solve this riddle:
what did the little boy say when

he was lost in the pyramid?

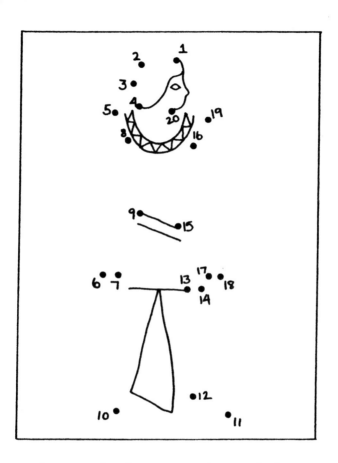

Connect the dots to see what might be
painted in an Egyptian tomb.

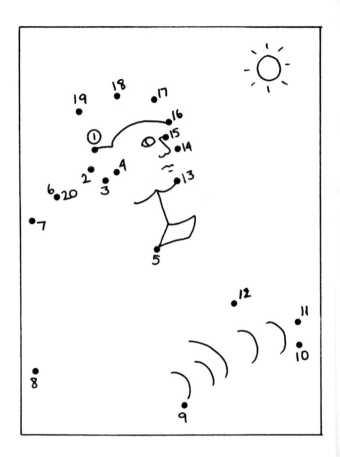

Connect the dots to reveal
a picture of a sphinx.

Solutions

page 3

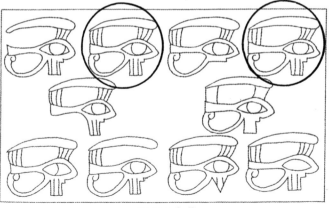

pages 4–5

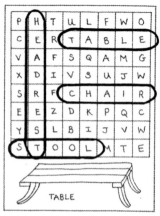

page 6

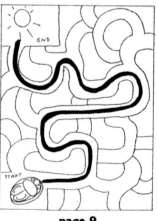

page 9

page 8

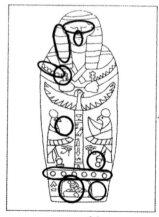

page 11

page 12

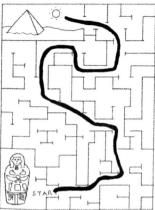

page 14

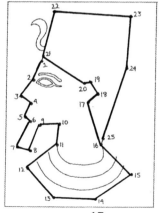

page 15

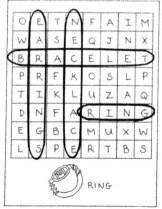

page 16

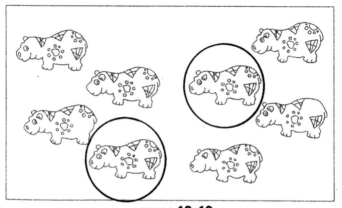

pages 18–19

page 20

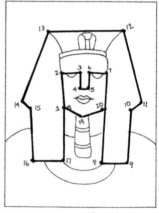

page 21

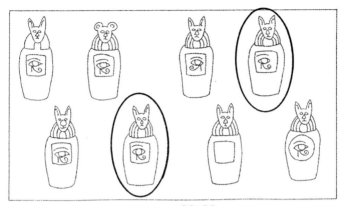

pages 22–23

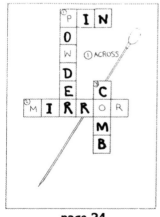

page 24

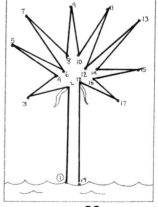

page 26

page 27

page 29

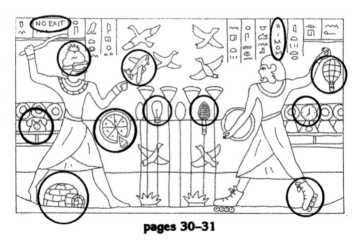

pages 30–31

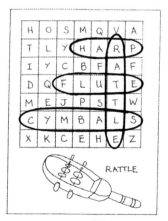

pages 32–33

page 34

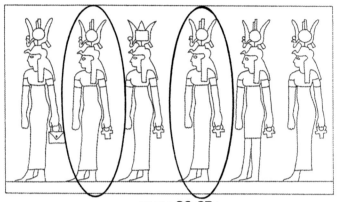

pages 36–37

page 39

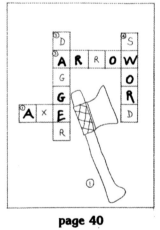

page 40

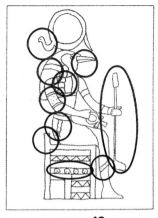

page 43

page 44

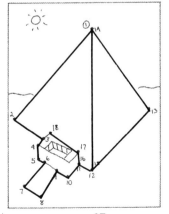

page 45

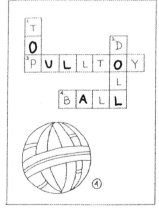

page 46

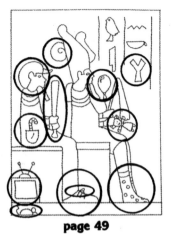

page 49

page 52

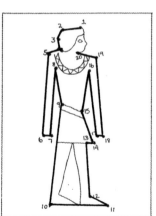

page 53

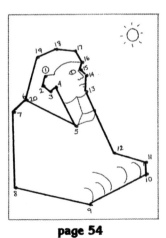

page 54